5 RULES FOR SURVIVNG THE COMING RECESSION (AND 5 MORE TO COME OUT ON TOP)

By: Randy Kent

TABLE OF CONTENTS

Inevitability Of Recession

The news is full of doom and gloom stories, enough to make you lose hope. We're headed towards a recession. We all know that, but what can you do to survive AND prepare your self, company or brand for success in the inevitable economic downturn?

Don't focus on today's recession - prepare for the recovery! Survival in the recession requires discipline and courage. Success in the recovery requires vision and commitment, right now.

To succeed, right now you need

✓ **Discipline**

✓ **Courage**

✓ **Vision**

✓ **Commitment**

TIDBITS FOR SMALL BUSINESS OWNERS

Keep investing in your marketing program at a similar or slightly higher percentage of your sales revenue or projected revenue (the actual dollar value may be less than your current spend however).

It's important not to expect the same results or ROI that you got before the recession - think of it as an investment in preparing your brand for the inevitable recovery. Your brand needs to be "top of mind" in the early stages in order to enjoy maximum benefits and growth once the economy recovers.

Become your own customer

If you're still doing some advertising (I hope you are) then you must make sure your investment generates maximum results by ensuring that your brand strategy is in line with your long-term vision. Ask yourself these questions:

- Are you talking to the right people? Make sure you are talking directly to your target market and using the right media titles, communication channels etc.

- Do you fully understand how your prospect makes purchase decisions? What do they value, what makes them buy from you and not your competitor? Without a clear understanding of these factors you're shooting in the dark.

- Does your message and offering effectively address the prospects needs, value system and buying criteria? You must match your value proposition to their needs - it's a marketing fundamental. Give them what they want, not what you think they should have!

There's a great saying that sums this up - "You can't be a bullfighter until you have been a bull".

RECOMMENDATION B

- Make a list of all customer "touch points" where your brand interacts with the market, your customers and prospects.
- Review and analyse the list and then strategise how you can make the experience of interacting with your brand and company more effective and memorable.

Turn your customers into disciples

How can you excite and delight your customers at zero cost? About 10 years ago I traveled to South Africa, where for many years the level of service across most industries, was at best, dismal. My last time there I was pleasantly surprised to find a huge improvement in service across all touchpoints.

I'm guessing the upcoming FIFA World Cup in 2010 had a lot to do with it, but the important thing is that I really enjoyed the retail service experience and how special I was made to feel. I now find myself telling everyone that asks about my trip, how great the service was (and not how bad the crime is). Now it didn't cost the businesses I frequented in my time there a cent, but it certainly added value to my experience of the "South Africa" brand. In fact, you could say I'm now a disciple by default.

Never forget that WOM (word of mouth) advertising is the most powerful form of promotion, and it costs nothing to generate, other than effort and discipline. In other words, you need to "out-service" your competitors!

Don't discount your product or service

A typical marketing response in a recession is to cut prices. Reducing prices in a recession necessitates a reduction in resource, ultimately leading to deterioration of service delivery. This is a downward death spiral!

Here are some remarkable (if not scary) numbers...

Roughly speaking, based on an initial profit margin of 33%, a 5% price cut requires around 15-20% increase in sales to make the same dollar profit (depending on whether you look at revenue or unit increase). More startlingly, a 15% price cut could require up to a 60% increase in sales to make the same dollar profit! Now 5% isn't exactly a show stopper and it's unlikely to do much for sales volumes. Even a 15% price drop won't generate additional sales revenues anything close to what is required to recover lost profit margin.

So if you were prepared to sacrifice 15% off your profit margin to get sales (typical recessionary discount strategy) then you'd be better off keeping prices at current levels and losing 60% of sales - the net financial result is the same. However, if you cut prices now you will find it much harder (maybe impossible) to lift them when the economy recovers. In effect, you erode your brand's value and trap yourself into a low-cost market position.

Price cuts may generate some short term gains, but they place you in a weak position to take advantage of or to maximise the inevitable economic recovery. The recovery is a given. It may take 12 months, it may take longer, but it WILL happen. How are you preparing your brand for it?

Agonize over your website

Your website should be a powerful sales lead generating

tool. To get the most out of your website investment there are a few important things you need to have in place:

- Your site must be optimized for effective search engine and Google results (also known as SEO). This is not a given and most sites are NOT optimized (good news for you). The key aspects required to be featured in Google are your URL page names, keyword relevance and density, meta tags and backlinks to your site. Without these, a high result in Google searches is not likely.

- Basic optimization of your website can be a very beneficial one-off investment. For what would be similar in cost to a small direct mail campaign, a medium sized newspaper ad or a decent Yellow Pages ad, you can turn your website into a powerful lead generating machine. The advantage is there are no recurring costs here (unless you want to further optimize your site).

- Does the site structure lend itself to generating visitor inquiries? Is it intuitive? Do you have a strong call-to-action? Is it easy to make an inquiry? All of these components are crucial in getting website visitors past the home page and into your catalogs and services.

- Who in your team responds to web inquiries and how quickly respond? This is a key "touch point" for your brand. Do you have someone who you've delegated customer service to, or are you tackling the issue yourself? I recently sent an email to the international consumer goods giant, SC Johnson regarding one of their products that didn't seem to be performing as well as it used to. The inquiry section of the website required me to download a Word template which I then had to populate, save onto my PC and email as an attachment! Honestly, you would have think they would have heard of online submit forms. It then took them about 3 weeks to reply, with the usual excuse that they have been so busy blah, blah, blah. So not only am I a bad advert for their poorly performing product, but I'm definitely NOT a disciple for their brand. Sadly, they have lost a golden opportunity to excite and delight me. Whatever your strategy, make sure it is simple and intuitive for your customers to get the information and reponses they need out of you.

So In Summary, Here Are The Key Success Factors For Marketing Your Brand In The Recession:

✓ **Invest in your brand**

✓ **Become your own customer**

✓ **Turn your customers into disciples**

✓ **Out-service your competitor (don't cut prices)**

✓ **Agonize over your website**

SURVIVING THE RECESSION

In past years, the negative impact of economic recession such as unemployment and high-priced goods greatly influenced the lives of many people. Recently, the issues relevant to economic recession are flooding news headlines and many people stand to suffer because of them. To survive the recession this time, all of us must not dwell on the problems that have caused it. It is here already, and time to take action. Let us all focus on finding solutions to the looming economic recession and assist each other in weathering this storm.

Economic recession means that our nation's economy is stagnant or going down for two consecutive quarters. The first quarter of the fiscal year is coming to an end, and to put it bluntly, it was a bloodbath. The path to surviving the recession starts with you. First, you should be finding a stable job that would likely survive the recession. This would include jobs related to education, health and public administration. On the other hand, avoid jobs that are associated with construction and retail because these rely on cash surplus in the economy.

If you have a job or other source of income, make sure that you allot a certain percentage of it towards building your savings. Learn to live below your means, so that if an income source of your household goes away, you will be able to sustain the lifestyle your accustomed to. Having a well-planned budget decreases the tendency to buy unnecessary items and ensures that at months end you will have made more than you've spent. Prioritize your needs over wants. Being practical nowadays will also allow you to avoid having unnecessary debt, and to stay on top of your finances. In times of recession it is beneficial to keep cash, as it allows you to avoid engaging yourself with debt, and the value of the dollar has been on the rise since the crash began. If you are already engaged with debt, prioritize paying it down as the interest rates will bury you. The Federal Reserve has cut interest rates twice, so refinancing your debt is definitely a route to consider in order to simplify your debt payments and save a little extra each month in interest.

You could also save some money if you will learn how to do household chores yourself that you usually pay others to do for you. Instead of going out to get food, or ordering from a fast food restaurant, learn how to cook your favorite meal and other simple items that are tasty and not time consuming. You could also study gardening, fixing of household items, and painting, among other household chores. Not only can these activities translate into saved money, but they can be fun, free ways to kill time that are free as well.

Setting these goals with the determination to adhere to and enact them will certainly help you to survive this recession. The nationwide effect of economic recession can be counteracted if each of us commits to making our own small and simple changes. After all, great things begin at the basic foundations of the society, which are our homes!

RULE 1. ELIMINATE EXCESSIVE OUTSTANDING DEBT

Financial stress is the number one contributor to divorce according to surveys taken around the United States. The anxiety that unpaid bills and accruing interest rates place on an individual can be overwhelming to the point of causing depression and other health and psychological ailments. Unfortunately, slipping into debt is made easy by a culture that prides itself on material belongings and instant gratification. To make matters worse, little to no educational resources are available to help people stay out of debt, save their money or better yet, invest it. This combination of factors creates a perfect storm for excess debts, possibly culminating in the filing of bankruptcy. If your personal finances sound similar to this description, it is time to get serious about taking steps eliminate your debt.

Any number of jokes can be aimed at a recklessly spending, middle class, materialist society, but at the end of the day, humor only helps so much. Instead, the first line approach should be education. To eliminate your debts you need to have the tools to guide you through the process.

The first tool is developing a balanced account of bills, income, and leftover finances. Once that equation has been drawn out, you will be able to see if your cash flow is in positive or negative territory. If your cashflow is negative, you will have to assess which bills can be eliminated first. For example, with the federal reserve lowering interest rates it's a great time to refinance your mortgage. Car payments, can be stopped by selling the car and purchasing one within your means. The same can be said for other material possessions you're indebted for owning. Common ones include laptops, televisions, and cell phones. Even if you have take a loss to sell an item like a car, it is better to stop the influx of bills until your income exceeds your costs. The objective is to generate a net positive monthly balance for the rest of your life.

The second action to take is to find a second or even a third job if necessary. This is not a popular stance to take, however, when compared with the stress of financial bleeding, a temporary extra job is a great solution. Working extra hours to eliminate debt, even if it's just one bill, can quickly turn your financial picture into a positive portrait. It also provides insurance against potential layoffs, furloughs, or cuts in hours that are common in times of recession. If you don't like the idea of dealing with another boss, you can try walking dogs, tutoring (in person or remotely), or getting involved in any other person to person or person to business service role.

The final effort you should take is to eliminate your credit card debt. Credit cards are considered toxic debt. Unlike a house payment, that presents an eventual return on investment, credit cards are empty debt. To eliminate your debt, you must erase credit card interest and stick to a well-built budget. Remember, the goal is to minimize monthly costs, and maximize monthly income. Eliminating debt in order from the most toxic, to least toxic is the most straightforward way to get closer to this goal.

RULE 2. FORTIFY YOUR SAVINGS

Increasing your income is a critical step in the Wealth Creation Formula. It will be difficult to become rich without the increase in your income. Once you have created an income flow. Find ways to increase it. This is different from going to get a second job, or starting a business. Here, I want you to increase the income from your current flow.

Don't lose focus on your first source. This is where people have the most to lose, but also the most to gain. They try to branch out too quickly. The sexiness of quitting their jobs drives them to look for other sources without perfecting their first source. In addition to fortifying your first source, increasing the cash flow associated takes skill. The learning process will help you later, when the appropriate time to scale your side income(s) reveals itself.

The Importance of Your First Stream

Your primary income source is your lifeline. This is why we want to increase it. All too often people start new business ventures and let the energy they dedicate to their primary income flow fizzle out. Remember your primary source pays the bills, keeps food on the table, and will fund future investments and ventures.

The movement to become your own boss is enticing. The road is paved with broke bosses and would be entrepreneurs. Starting a side hustle is the correct thing to do. But please do not make this move before you secure and increase your first flow. Your first flow funds your entire lifestyle. You can't forget that.

How can you increase your income now through your primary source? How can you bring more money in with what you are already doing? Can you offer marketing services and clientele to your employer for commission? What other duties can you perform around the workplace to get more money coming into the company, and accordingly into your bank account?

You can increase your pay, by increasing your value to your customer, and employer. Have you looked into ways to earn more money in your current position? Here are some examples:

Food service workers, waiters, and waitresses can improve their communication skills to get higher tips. Uber, Lyft, Taxi, and Delivery Drivers can improve their service for more tips. They can put up signs that remind people to tip. Also, rideshare drivers can drive more to earn bonuses. They can also participate in referral or affiliate programs to earn more money recruiting more riders and drivers.

Sales and Commission people can earn more money by doing learning for to do the financing side of whatever they're selling to go along with their sales skills. If the customer doesn't choose to buy from you, you could refer the customer to a competitor or fellow salesmen and earn a referral fee.

Blue Collar/Union Worker can increase their skill set to learn other jobs and use their seniority to get extra work. Is their overtime available for you to take to increase that current flow?

No Opportunities to Increase?

Now there are some instances where you can not increase your income. This is where you invest in yourself. Instead of hopping on the next get rich trend. Invest in learning a skill like sales and marketing. Learn how to turn your current skill set into dollars.

What does Increasing Your Income Look Like?

Here is what increasing your income flow looks like:

Let's say you are an Uber driver. Driving is your main source. Now one way to increase your income is to drive longer hours. You can drive for 12 hours per day with Uber. Next, you can increase your tips by having a clean car, communicating well, and having signage that reminds people to tip. Then you can recruit other people and get a referral fee.

With Bonuses and tips alone a rideshare driver could earn up to $400 extra per week. This is how you increase your current income flow. The key is to find opportunities with your current job or business. It saves you time, and while there is a learning curve, once you've developed the skillset you can take it with you into any future business endeavors. You are already an expert in what you are doing. Find ways to get paid more to do it.

Don't Become Satisfied with Your First Flow

Once you master your first flow don't become satisfied. Don't compare yourself with other people because you are doing better. The goal is wealth creation. One income stream will never make you truly wealthy. On the other hand, you've fortified your key income source and now you can create other streams because your main stream is strong, and you're fortified against layoffs, and hour reductions if and when they begin.

You should never let your wealth depend on one income. Now that this is fortified and growing it is time to find a second source. The second source is another flow. It is not replacing your first stream. It is adding to your income. Branching out takes courage and skills. If you have increased your income from your first flow chanes are that you have developed some basic self-marketing skills, even if you haven't realized it.

RULE 3. IMPROVE YOUR HIRABILITY

It is important to understand that the most straightforward way to improve a business is by hiring the right employees. The team that an organization has supporting its goals can make or break the entire operation in times of financial crisis. Members of the staff manufacture or distribute products and provide services to the customers. A companies employees are the ones that build the reputation of a brand through a dedication to quality, and positive interactions with customers. It is essential that you become indispensable to your organization, regardless of your role in its structure.

Be the right hire that benefits your organization in ways above and beyond your job description. Help to improve employee morale in hard times, as being a positive force in the company alone can help you avoid being let go during staff turnover events. This in turn means that you end up keeping your main income source when things are pointing south. If you raise the bar in terms of productivity and push all the members of the team to a higher standard of efficiency, you maximize the companies return on their investment in you. These things won't go unnoticed, especially in times of trouble. Whether you are the CFO of a company or work the brake press at a metal fabrication plant, you can work hard to be the best at what you do.

Focus Your Efforts on Qualities That Benefit the Establishment

Decide what the goals of your establishment are. The skills and qualities you take time to acquire must support these objectives. For example, if your business is heavily sales oriented, you need to focus on being friendly and outgoing. If you are primarily involved in auto repairs, you must have good customer relations skills as well, but the technical expertise would be their chief quality.

The design of the company will determine who will complement it. In turn, being a person who aligns themself with that design can propel your success in times of recession more than at any other time. In the long term, your company will lose money if they pick the wrong individuals, so consistently proving that you were the right choice at the right time will solidify your role.

Be Open Minded to Your Companies Changing Needs

Make sure that you're a person who is trainable. This will add value to you as an asset for years to come. If you are a person who is unwilling to learn new skills, you will always be limited by the amount of knowledge that you have. When you do want to expand in certain areas, your past flexibility will be remembered, and the company will be more willing to provide you with opportunity for advancement. This is a great habit to develop, as it can help you build a sustainable feedback loop of hard work resulting in opportunity.

When economic tragedy strikes, a company's needs can change drastically. It will be the people with functioning working knowledge of the entire operation, and the most specialized individuals who will be kept around. Tough times require fluidity in a company's staff, and the ability to maintain a standard of operation, even with less manpower. If you want to help your establishment to grow to a certain level, where it can be recession proof, so you can be recession proof, then you must become a person with the abilities needed to add value within the new paradigm.

Choose Skills and Experience That Give You an Edge over the Competition

You do not want replicate qualities that are already present in your organization. You should carefully analyze the weaknesses and strengths of your current team, and optimize your skills and mindset to interact in the best way possible with the other members of your team or organization. Try to be a person who looks for positive results and uses their talents well. Be driven to produce when goals are set. Be a person who is confident in their abilities and is genuinely interested in the assignment that you've been given.

If you want to know how to improve a business, it is important to observe your competitors. Look at the kind of staff that they have. By observing the members of their team, you can determine what qualities you want or need on your own team. You can also deduce the types of people and personalities that you do not want in your organization. If you are an excellent employee, you will be given the freedom to manage yourself and your own teams and your organization will know that you're not a person who is satisfied with mediocrity.

RULE 4. TRACK YOUR FINANCES (ELIMINATE UNNECESSARY SPENDING)

If you suspect you are overspending, you need to take the time to sit down and figure out exactly where your money is going each month. Saving is an important habit that needs to be cultivated over time, and it's a great place to start. Even if you're overspending, if you're making sure to save regardless, you're already ahead of the game. So, what now? Fortunately, technology has made it easier than ever to track your finances. Analyzing on what you spend is the best way to avoid overspending. How do you track your expenses? I personally used a manual process via an excel spreadsheet during my college years, when my finances were much simpler, but now I use Mint by Intuit, as it does all of the budgeting and calculates my net monthly income for me. There are a myriad of apps to use, or if you prefer to have more control, you can utilize a more manual process, either through a spreadsheet app like excel, or manually in a notebook.

If this is your first time, it can be awkward. This is especially true if you are already an adult. Good habits of financial awareness are not easy to develop, and many people never get into this process because they're genuinely too afraid to look. Nevertheless, it is never too late.

To get the dice rolling, get your hands on the following:

- Your recent pay slips

- Tax documents (especially the returns)

- Banking bills, payment records (offline and online)

- Registers for checkbooks (this includes cancelled checks) and debit card transaction history

- Credit card bills

Compile the documents necessary to keep track of 12 months period of spending.

If your spending patterns are consistent throughout, you can reduce it to a 6 month time frame. Whenever you make a huge purchase, be sure to include the month when the expenses occurred and account for it.

Cash payments are hard to track

This is because they do not have a paper trail. How do you solve this? Easy. Record everything you buy with cash during a week time period. I simply use the notes app on my iphone, but you can keep them tracked in a journal, or input them directly into the finance tracking app of your choice in real time. Sometimes, you might get lazy, fall behind and estimate the amount. This is perfectly ok, but I generally suggest overestimating what you've spent, and underestimating what you've brought in.

Label your expenditures into useful categories

Classify them into sections like taxes, house, food, transportation, lifestyle, debt repayments, leisure, personal care, health care, insurance and so on. Once you have a grasp on where your spending is directed, you can work out a budget you're willing to stick to. Too many people set unrealistic budgets, and then beat themselves up for going overbudget. The best thing you can do is allocate a larger portion of your income to your budget, and adhere to it.

RULE 5. DON'T PANIC

One of the most important things to remember in trying times is don't panic. I know that might sound a little easier said than done. But if you have yourself all worked up it could cause you to have a panic or anxiety attack and neither of those are good when it comes to surviving a recession.

First of all you need to know that it is going to hurt, there is no getting around that aspect of a recession. What you can do is mentally prepare yourself for it. Keep in mind that if you've taken the right steps, and you're working to increase your net income, you will be alright. The worst thing you can do is pull all your investments and savings. While things will be tough, your investments will return to market value, and those savings are for your future. As tempting as liquidating your savings and assets may be, a recession presents the greatest opportunity for financial gains. It is the time to be saving with intentions of investing once things start pointing upwards. More wealth is generated during recessions than any other time throughout economic history. As long as you don't panic, and stick to the plan, you will set yourself up to achieve wealth you may never have imagined previously.

COMING OUT ON TOP

Every individual in this world has a dream to achieve success in their life. While the qualities which define success are different for everybody, they all revolve around the idea of freedom. It is unfortunate that not many are able to achieve their dreams, or even attain the freedom required to pursue them. Are you among the people interested in becoming successful, in becoming free? If you are, then this section will show you the five most effective rules on how to turn an economic recession into unprecedented financial growth.

What does it mean to achieve success in life?

No doubt every individual is unique, and as a result becoming successful means different things to everybody. It becomes easier for you to understand how to become successful when you are able to comprehend what success means to you.

If you know what success is, why have you not become successful yet? Yes, this is a very sensitive issue, but you'll be stuck in place unless you take the time to reflect on what's holding you back. Why are certain people successful and others not? Is it something in our past or genetics that prevent us from excelling in life? Or Is it simply because you do not know how to become successful?

Truly, certain aspects of our lives cannot be changed and some aspects are awfully hard to modify. Our personalities drive us toward different ventures and allow us to excel in different roles. Locking down your own personality traits and discovering how to best utilize them can make all the difference in your pursuit of success.

Most people in the world quote some excuses as the basis for their inability to be successful in life such as lack of money, lack of time and talent. An economic recession can in many ways be the great equalizer regarding these factors. Will you stop making excuses and use the opportunity to pursue your goals, or will you cower from the potential and treat the crash as another obstacle between you and your goals?

Steps To Become Successful in Life

What are YOUR excuses for not been able to become successful in life? Be very honest with yourself. To become successful in life there are really just a handful of straight forward rules to follow. What are these rules which will allow you to become successful in the wake of financial crisis?

RULE 1. BUY PRECIOUS METALS

Buying precious metal is a great way to bring diversify your holdings, especially when the economy is going under. Historically, the stock markets and precious metals have maintained an inverse relationship. As one increases the other decreases and vice versa. With this, investing in precious metals can be a very delicate decision which does have some risk as you never know when there will be fluctuations in the prices. It is also one of the smartest decisions you can make. It carries the same risks as all kinds of investments you make, but it's less difficult with metals as you can see the factors that may cause any change and you can make your investing propositions accordingly. Gold price depends upon on the performance of the US Dollar and the Euro. This makes people feel secure to invest in gold, as long as they are diligent in tracking the spot price vs the broader financial market conditions and health indicators. Metals are one of the best ways to safeguard your investments. The price of metals shoots up if the market is hit by any type of crisis. Natural crises such as a tsunami or an earthquake often lead to increase in the prices of metals, as well financial crisis, be it a correction, a recession, or something worse.

Buying precious metal is a much better idea today than tomorrow. The price of gold is more expensive today than it was last month, and as the markets continue to slide it is only getting more expensive. The crumbling stock market has made many citizens concerned about investing their hard earned money in ETFs and fortune 500 companies. Therefore it is encouraged to invest in hard assets like gold and silver, to hedge against a potential crash.

The rising prices of gold have led the people to opt for different options to choose from when it comes to buying precious metal. Investors are taking interest in metals like silver, copper, platinum, and palladium. As the traders and investors make changes in their shares it affects the spot price of all of these metals. Due to the increase in the mining of silver specifically and a dwindling silver supply, market and financial analysts are becoming more interested in the prices of silver, more so than gold even. Investors presume that silver will outplace other financial commodities, which is why I've chosen to stockpile a large amount of it myself.

If you are looking for making your own investments then buying precious metal gives you exciting opportunities to stay in control of your own finances. With so many alternatives in the investment market it may be difficult for you to choose the right options, so you will definitely want to have a detailed study about the market position before you make any investments.

RULE 2. DIVERSIFY IN ACCORDANCE WITH WHEN YOU WANT TO RETIRE

If you want to have a safe and secure financial life during your retirement, then you have to think about investing. When you are planning your investment strategy for retirement, you have to take into account several factors. While it is complex to do this planning, it will give you peace of mind during your golden years.

There is no fixed age for retirement, and as such everybody has different financial goals in mind. However, one thing is for sure- that anyone who retires has to be ready to live without full time employment. At the same time, the age that you retire at will determine how many years you will have to survive without full time employment. Hence, your investment should be such that it can handle all potential financial liabilities for those years, and hopefully produce more income for you on a regular basis.

If you are planning investments for retirement, it is best to opt for safe investment vehicles. One of the first things that you should do is open a high yield bank account and ensure that you deposit money into that account every month without fail. While the interest may not be high for savings account, you will be gradually building a nest egg for yourself over the years. Now most people would just save and hope they have enough at age 65. My suggestion is that you continually use this nest egg to purchase assets that will provide paychecks every month.

Another way to invest for retirement is by opting for Certificates of Deposits, popularly known as CDs. Here you will be 'lending' money for a fixed period of time to the issuer of the certificate and when the certificate matures, you will get the principal amount as well as the interest on it. Usually it is advisable to have laddered investments so that right through your retirement, each CD keeps maturing and providing you with much needed income.

Another safe option for investing for retirement is bonds. Just like CDs, even bonds mature after a fixed period of time and the bond issuer returns the principal amount and interest on that amount.

Today, a lot of people are also opting for mutual funds. This is a safer option for retirement saving compared to the stock market. While the stock market is extremely volatile, mutual funds allow you diversify your investment portfolio without being hindered by the volatility.

If you are uncomfortable with planning your investment for retirement, you can hire the services of an asset allocation company. These companies will plan your investment after taking into consideration all your financial needs and retirement goals. However, make sure that you find a reliable and trustworthy company or individual to handle your funds.

RULE 3. USE REAL ESTATE TO BUILD LONG TERM WEALTH

Gaining financial knowledge can put you ahead and help you get out of the rat race of life faster than any job could. Something most schools don't teach our kids but is very necessary to be able to get ahead financially, is the power of investment, and the purpose of cash flow generating investments. I would recommend everyone to read Rich Dad Poor Dad Book for your financial education, especially if your interested investing in real estate.

First, get your education in the area in which you want to invest. When it comes to cash flow in the long term, real estate is king. I would recommend starting with a small multifamily house to rent out. It is important to host multiple families if possible, that way if you lose one tenant, you're not stuck covering the entirety of a mortgage thanks to the other tenants in your building. I like to buy and hold property and have the rent payment cover all the costs involved in owning the building. The insurance, property tax, maintenance costs, mortgage payment, advertising, and if you pay the utilities they should be covered too. Otherwise you have to come up with money every month to pay for expenses not covered and end up having to work harder or longer. You want to work smarter not harder. Get the education needed to gain sustainable long term wealth.

After getting an education you need to go out there and look for properties to buy, figure out what area you want to invest in. You can greatly reduce your risk by knowing which properties are good and which properties are bad.

Buy in a good neighborhood, find out what rents are in the area. When you find a house you are interested in you will need to do your homework, does it make sense financially? Is the market flooded with houses to rent? That's not all bad but your house may sit empty for a while. Do a home inspection of the property ext. Take action, talk to people who know more about the are than you do. Doing your part in finding out about the area and the property.

Investing in real estate can be very rewarding if done right. It does, however, involve Investing considerable amounts time to educate and money to really take action. Many people say they don't want to be a landlord because they are afraid of getting a call to fix the toilet or get a call in the middle of the night that the furnace is broke. You don't have to be able to fix a toilet or the furnace, but you do have to have a team of people you work with. It's crucial to have skilled contractors you can trust, and if you find a good one be sure to maintain a positive relationship with them. Others fear the tenants may destroy the place. You can reduce the risk of this happening by doing your part of thorough background checks and purposeful discussions with potential tenants so you can clearly define expectations. Talk to their prior landlords to find out what type of renters they are. Did they pay their rent on time? Were they generally tidy people? You are well within your rights to figure out exactly who you'll be renting your space to, and you would be foolish not to do just that.

RULE 4. DON'T BE AFRAID TO VOLUNTEER (BUILDING COMMUNITY)

Success in times of recession requires a team effort and in order for individuals to be successful they must be able to communicate effectively with their friends and neighbors. In spite of our best efforts, people generally fear discussion regarding finances, especially when they are on the losing side of an economic collapse. That's why it can provide great benefit to show up and help your community when the opportunity presents itself.

Hard times befall everybody, and almost never conveniently. Being an active member of your community will provide you the chance to help those around you when hard times hit them. Difficult times often are a powerful reminder of how interconnected we really are, even in todays environment of digital isolationism.

In addition, you can never really know when the economic downturn will affect you. Regardless of whether you follow the rules laid out throughout this book, nobody is impervious. If you remain an active member of your community when you're on the winning side of things, your neighbors may very well step up to lend a helping hand when you're in need. That is the power of community- real people providing other real people a leg to stand on when they need it most.

Whether you choose to donate to charity, deliver pro bono groceries on the weekend, or even just attend local town halls ot voice your opinion, there are many ways to stay active and stay involved.

RULE 5. BUILD THAT SECOND SOURCE OF INCOME

If you've ever thought that maybe a traditional 9-5 desk job isn't right for your professional life, then it's time to learn more about diversifying your income source and finding ways to produce income doing whatever thing(s) you enjoy most. Believe it or not an economic recession is arguably the best time to build out your second source of income. Often getting started takes a good deal of legwork, and research, but when you're trying to spend less and save more, finding ways either online or in your community to make additional money can be a fun challenge to take on. It is often very low cost to start (educational materials, website, small marketing campaign, etc.) and if you have taken steps to solidify yourself as an integral component at your primary career it is the greatest opportunity you'll have to get after it. Competition levels decrease, and the whole world operates at a discount in times of recession. While it's not the business model I think people should follow during recessionary periods, I do strongly believe it is worth taking advantage of.

Maybe you've had a desk job before, or maybe you're reading this while trying not to count the seconds until the workday is over. Maybe you even like your current job, but you're interested in developing new strategies for marketing yourself, taking advantage of your broad skill set, and earning a little extra cash on the side. Whatever interest you might have in creating multiple sources of income, you've come to the right place.

The most important thing to consider when devising a

method for creating new income sources is whether or not you have a skill that you're underutilizing. Odds are you probably do, and in the interest of examples, let's pretend for a moment that you're a graphic designer working on salary at an ad agency, and completing whatever projects are tossed in your general direction by management. Let's say that right now, work at your firm entails a great deal of computer drafting. Sure you know you're way around the software and no one has ever complained about your results, but in your heart of hearts, you know that you're work drawing freehand to create logos and designs is your most unique skill. Although you certainly have skill and can add value if you've landed this job, chances are there's still more you could do to more fully utilize your capabilities.

This is the point at which you must consider your options for specialization. The fact is, you have a skill and you need to let the world know about. By promoting your work and creating a brand and reputation, you can leverage your talent into a client list who will pay you, not your agency. to create hand drawn logos that inspire and help build success for your clientele. This is especially true in a recession, as companies are more open to finding more affordable, local options than they are when the worlds major corporations are all on the uptick.

Maybe you LOVE your job, and you're thinking about using your generous salary for something other than lining the walls of your savings account. If this sounds like you, then it's time to make your money start to work for you. Consider investing in a number of assets that can bring in extra money today. We discussed real estate earlier, but you can also purchase a functioning e-commerce store, an android or iOS app that has been selling well, or dividend paying stocks that will provide quarterly checks dependent on the number of shares you own.

All of these options become more realistic to pursue when the economy is in a full downturn, if you know where to look and how to take advantage. I hope that this book has provided you value in the form of the confidence needed to go out and take on the recession with your head held high, and a plan in place.

BOOKS BY THIS AUTHOR

Bring Your Bills Down First: A Step By Step Guide To Making More Money Off Of Your Home

Bring Your Bills Down First provides its readers with a fresh look at their personal finances and where it can be improved. The book focuses on residential energy consumption, where those costs can be cut, and how to invest that money properly. It helps readers to understand that SAVED money and MADE money are one in the same. By providing specific examples, and a tried and proven 3- phase plan, this book provides the average homeowner with the knowledge that big solar and electric generation companies keep from them. Make a couple small changes, grow your savings, and start making investments that will make an impact on your bills, and climate change.

5 Rules For Surviving The Coming Recession (And 5 More To Come Out On Top)

www.ingramcontent.com/pod-product-compliance
Lightning Source LLC
Chambersburg PA
CBHW030544220526
45463CB00007B/2979